D0917892

A DORLING KINDERSLEY BOOK

First American Edition, 1992
10 9 8 7 6 5 4 3 2 1
Published in the United States by Dorling Kindersley, Inc.,
232 Madison Avenue, New York, New York 10016

For Sam

ISBN 1-56458-106-3
Library of Congress
Catalog Card Number 92-52802

Color reproduction by Dot Gradations
Printed in Singapore by Tien Wah Press Ltd

Prickly
ANIMALS

Illustrated by
Kenneth Lilly

Written by
Angela Wilkes

DORLING KINDERSLEY, INC.
NEW YORK

Contents

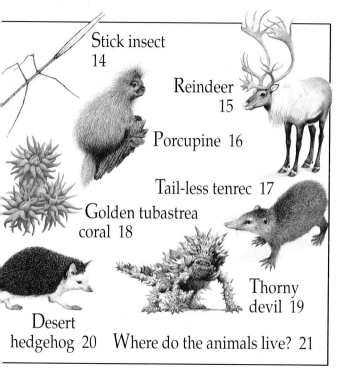

Hedgehog
The spiny hedgehog rolls up into a prickly ball when danger is near.

8

Spiny anteater
This anteater digs down into the soil
to hide from its enemies.

9

Marine iguana
The marine iguana is the only lizard in the world that swims and feeds in the ocean.

Tuatara
The male tuatara raises the
spines along his back to frighten
off attackers.

11

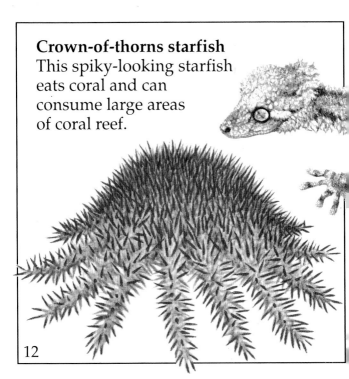

Crown-of-thorns starfish
This spiky-looking starfish eats coral and can consume large areas of coral reef.

12

Leaf-tailed gecko
The gecko's shape makes it hard for other animals to spot it among the forest leaves.

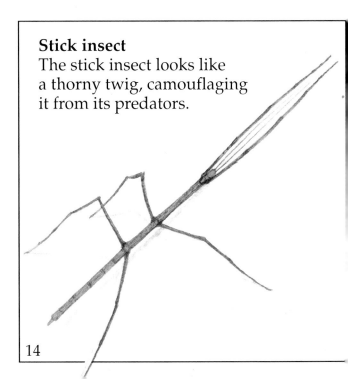

Stick insect
The stick insect looks like a thorny twig, camouflaging it from its predators.

14

Reindeer
Male reindeer fight with their large, pointed antlers. The winner leads the herd.

15

Porcupine
This animal's furry coat
hides thousands of
spines that stick
out when it is
frightened.

16

Reindeer
Male reindeer fight with their large, pointed antlers. The winner leads the herd.

15

Porcupine
This animal's furry coat hides thousands of spines that stick out when it is frightened.

Tail-less tenrec
The tail-less tenrec raises
its spines and hisses
to frighten away
enemies.

17

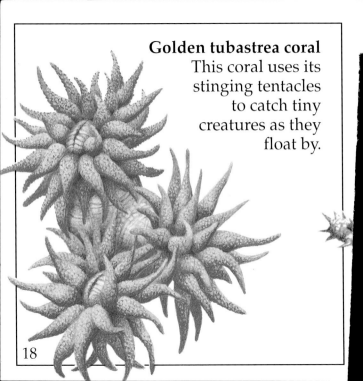

Golden tubastrea coral
This coral uses its stinging tentacles to catch tiny creatures as they float by.

18

Thorny devil
This spiky lizard lives in the desert.
It drinks the dew that
collects on its
skin at night.

Desert hedgehog
This hedgehog has long legs to keep
its body away from the hot sand.

20

Where do the animals live?

Hedgehog
European woodlands

Spiny anteater
Australia

Marine iguana
Galapagos Islands

Tuatara
New Zealand

Crown-of-thorns starfish
Great Barrier Reef, off
Australia

Leaf-tailed gecko
Australian rain forests

Stick insect
Madagascar

Reindeer
Arctic regions

Porcupine
Forests of North
America

Tail-less tenrec
Madagascar

Golden tubastrea coral
Great Barrier Reef, off
Australia

Thorny devil
Australian Outback

Desert hedgehog
Sahara desert, northern
Africa